DO GORILLAS EAT BANANAS?

HUW LEWIS JONES
EXPEDITION LEADER

SAM CALDWELL
WILDLIFE ARTIST

CONTENTS

GREAT APE ADVENTURE!	4
INTO THE RAINFOREST	6
TIME FOR A MAP	8
KNOW YOUR APES	10
THE GREAT APES	12
ANCIENT ANCESTORS	14
CHIMP COUSINS	16
FRUITY FEAST	18
WATCH OUT	20
FAMILY MATTERS	22
MOM KNOWS BEST	24
FIELD WORK	26
SCREEN TIME	28
BEAUTIFUL BRAINS	30
HANDY SKILLS	32
LISTEN UP	34
CLEVER AND COOL	36
BIG THREATS	38
TROUBLED TIMES	40
HAPPY ALONE	42
FINDING HOPE	44
APE WORDS	46
INDEX	47

GREAT APE ADVENTURE!

Are you ready for an expedition?

Welcome fellow apes! Are you ready to join us as we trek high into mountain forests and through hot, steamy jungles to meet different types of apes in their natural environment?

Can you imagine being an orangutan or a chimpanzee? Swinging through the trees all day may sound like fun, but these wonderful animals face a lot of threats too. Together we'll discover what life is really like for apes, and what we can do to protect them.

We are family!

In this book we will concentrate on the "great apes"—a family of primates known as "hominids" that today includes eight surviving species: two types of gorilla, chimpanzees, bonobos, three types of orangutan, and us . . . modern humans.

What do I need?

We're heading somewhere hot and wet, so a raincoat and hat are essential. Remember to bring a journal to draw and make notes about the interesting things you see. Binoculars are handy, too. Don't forget a snack or two, but please don't feed the animals!

Legendary apes

Apes of all kinds have captured our imaginations for hundreds of years. They continue to cause strong feelings—from fear to fascination, and even love. Many people around the world are now doing their best to help these remarkable animals. And you can too.

INTO THE RAINFOREST

Would you like to meet a chimpanzee?

If you've been lucky enough to see a chimpanzee in real life it was probably in a zoo, right? But wouldn't it be amazing to see one in its natural habitat? Most great apes live in tropical rainforests. Whether up in their branches, relaxing in the shade, or eating their fruit, among the trees is an ape's favorite place to be.

Hanging around

Though they have a lot in common, not all apes share the same habitat. Adult gorillas very rarely climb trees, preferring to hang out in the bushes and undergrowth, whereas orangutans spend most of their time high up in the branches.

Jungle sounds

Rainforests can be noisy places. The loud screams of apes around dawn and dusk can sound particularly alarming. Don't worry though, it's just their way of communicating with each other. Chimpanzees like to chatter and hoot, but gorillas are generally very quiet animals. Male orangutans make loud, booming calls, which can be heard over a mile away.

Stolen lives

For hundreds of years, apes and monkeys of all kinds have been hunted, captured, and sold as pets. Sadly, even though this is now illegal, thousands of apes are still being taken from the wild every year.

New knowledge

Researchers are learning new things about apes. We now know that they are incredibly clever communicators, and many live closely together and create strong bonds. Some apes will even die to protect each other.

TIME FOR A MAP

So, where do apes live?

Most great apes are found across Central Africa. Orangutans only live in the forests of Sumatra and Borneo, which are islands in Asia. And, of course, the most numerous of the great apes—humans—are found on every continent, in every country.

EASTERN GORILLA   WESTERN GORILLA

Gorilla differences

There are two main species of gorilla—western and eastern. Some eastern gorillas live high up in the mountains. They have longer hair than other gorillas because of how cold and wet it gets! Did you know, some adult western gorillas also have red hair on the top of their heads?

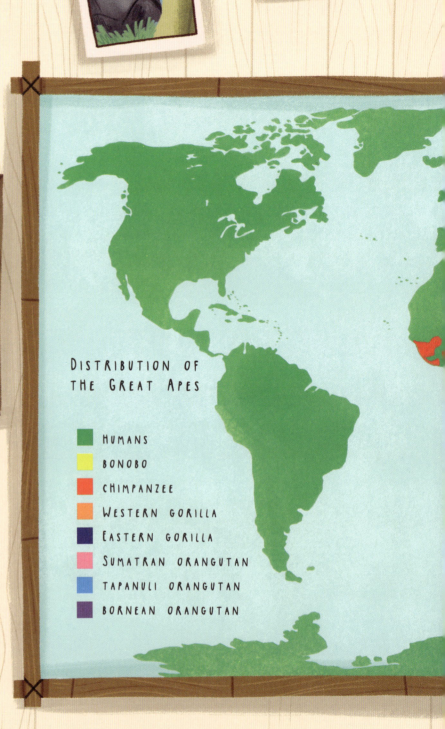

DISTRIBUTION OF THE GREAT APES

- HUMANS
- BONOBO
- CHIMPANZEE
- WESTERN GORILLA
- EASTERN GORILLA
- SUMATRAN ORANGUTAN
- TAPANULI ORANGUTAN
- BORNEAN ORANGUTAN

Wondrous nature

Every animal is special. So far, biologists have described over two million species of living things here on Earth, but there could be many more that have yet to be found and named—maybe even as many as ten million!

Just one planet

Today there are more than eight billion humans on our amazing planet. This is incredible—but also worrying. Natural habitats, including forests and jungles, are being destroyed as our population grows, including some where other apes live!

Long lives

A gorilla typically lives for about thirty-five years, though some have been known to live up to fifty years in sanctuaries. The oldest known orangutan is thought to be more than sixty years old! She lives in a zoo in Germany.

KNOW YOUR APES
Who's in the family?

Apes, monkeys, and humans all belong to the same big group—or "order"—of animals known as primates. Primate means "top animal" and was the name given to the group by scientist Carl Linnaeus over two hundred years ago. He created a naming system for animals, which is still used today.

Primates are a huge group that includes a lot of other mammals too, such as lemurs from Madagascar, and tiny tarsiers, which can be found hiding in forests in Asia. All primates have big brains, pretty good eyesight, and the ability to grasp things with their hands.

Monkey business

Apes are not monkeys. Almost all monkeys have tails, but apes do not. Apes are also bigger and more intelligent than monkeys. Somewhere in between the apes and monkeys are animals called gibbons.

WESTERN GORILLA
(*Gorilla gorilla*)

CHIMPANZEE
(*Pan troglodytes*)

BONOBO
(*Pan paniscus*)

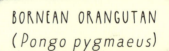

BORNEAN ORANGUTAN
(*Pongo pygmaeus*)

Double good
The western gorilla's scientific name is easy to remember. He's so good they named him twice: *Gorilla gorilla*!

IUCN Red List

Scientists are keeping a careful watch over all the different types of apes to make sure they're safe. Look for this symbol to see which species are most in need of our help.

Go fast gibbon
Gibbons are known as "small apes" because they are smaller than the great apes. They can walk on two legs on the ground, and have very long arms—twice the length of their bodies. They are incredible acrobats, and can swing through the trees faster than any other mammal.

HUMAN
(*Homo sapiens*)

LAR GIBBON
(*Hylobates lar*)

Scientific names
Every living thing on Earth that humans discover is given a unique scientific name consisting of two words in Latin, which are italicized. This naming system is the same all around the world, which helps people who speak different languages talk about animals without getting too mixed up.

The first word in a scientific name is the animal's genus and the second is its species. Animals that share the same genus are closely related. For example, the bonobo and the chimpanzee share the genus *Pan*. They look very similar but are now recognized as separate species.

THE GREAT APES

WESTERN GORILLA

Gorilla gorilla

Western gorillas are smaller than eastern gorillas and have reddish-brown foreheads.

WHERE? Central Africa

HOW MANY? 360,000*

IUCN RED LIST STATUS: Critically endangered

EASTERN GORILLA

Gorilla beringei

These rare gorillas live in mountain forests. Their hair is longer and thicker than western gorillas' hair.

WHERE? Central and East Africa

HOW MANY? Fewer than 3,000*

IUCN RED LIST STATUS: Critically endangered

CHIMPANZEE

Pan troglodytes

Chimpanzees are very adaptable and can be found in both the forest and mixed savannah.

WHERE? West and Central Africa

HOW MANY? 170,000–300,000*

IUCN RED LIST STATUS: Endangered

BONOBO

Pan paniscus

Easily confused with chimpanzees, bonobos weren't recognized as a separate species until 1929.

WHERE? Democratic Republic of the Congo, Central Africa

HOW MANY? 10,000–20,000*

IUCN RED LIST STATUS: Endangered

SUMATRAN ORANGUTAN

Pongo abelii

These apes seem to form closer social bonds than Bornean orangutans.

WHERE? Sumatra

HOW MANY? Fewer than 14,000*

IUCN RED LIST STATUS: Critically endangered

BORNEAN ORANGUTAN

Pongo pygmaeus

Orangutan species can be hard to tell apart, but Bornean orangutans tend to have slightly shorter and darker hair than their cousins in Sumatra.

WHERE? Borneo

HOW MANY? Fewer than 100,000*

IUCN RED LIST STATUS: Critically endangered

TAPANULI ORANGUTAN

Pongo tapanuliensis

These orangutans were only recognized as a separate species in 2017. They live in a small area of South Tapanuli in North Sumatra, over sixty miles away from other orangutans.

WHERE? North Sumatra

HOW MANY? Fewer than 800*

IUCN RED LIST STATUS: Critically endangered

HUMAN

Homo sapiens

Highly adaptable and less hairy than other apes (well . . . most of us!).

WHERE? Every country in the world

HOW MANY? Eight billion and rising!

IUCN RED LIST STATUS: Not on the list

*ESTIMATED

ANCIENT ANCESTORS
Were there dino-apes?

Sixty-six million years ago, an asteroid smashed into Earth and wiped out the big dinosaurs and many other predators. With fewer creatures trying to eat them, small mammals began to thrive and eventually evolved in a wide variety of ways. In the forests, many animals took to the trees, where it was often much safer, and fruit and nuts could be found.

Climate crisis

As apes and monkeys dispersed across the continents, they evolved in many different ways to adapt to new environments. Although apes have triumphed over thousands of years of climate change, the speed of current warming conditions and forest destruction pose a new threat to all species.

PURGATORIUS

The earliest known proto-primate.

WEIGHT: About 1.5 oz.

WHERE: North America

WHEN: Sixty-three million years ago

OREOPITHECUS

This ancient primate lived in swampy habitats.

WEIGHT: About 90 lb.

WHERE: Italy

WHEN: Nine million years ago

The first primates

Nowadays, finding fossils in the ground helps researchers to learn more about animal history. The first primate-like mammals are referred to as "proto-primates." Evidence from fossils tells us they were somewhat similar to squirrels in size and appearance!

CHIMP COUSINS

Are humans related to apes?

"Are we monkeys?" "Was my great-grandma a gorilla?" I'm often asked these questions in schools. In a way, the answer is . . . yes! If we go back a very long way, then we are all related. All great apes share a common ancestor, a primate, from over twenty million years ago.

Human evolution

Researchers still don't know exactly when the first humans evolved. One of the earliest known is *Homo habilis*, or "handy man," who lived about two million years ago in eastern and southern Africa. Others include *Homo erectus*, or "upright man," who could be found in Africa, China, and Indonesia about 1.9 million to 100,000 years ago, before going extinct.

Ancient hunters

Homo neanderthalensis, often called Neanderthals, were probably the closest relatives to modern humans. They lived in Europe and parts of Asia between 400,000 and 40,000 years ago. They were skilled at hunting large Ice Age animals like bison and woolly rhinos, and archaeologists now think that they communicated with language and had their own culture.

Shared DNA

Evidence suggests that humans and chimpanzees diverged from a common ancestor about six million years ago. Today, humans and chimps share 98.8 percent of their DNA! Though humans also share roughly sixty percent of their DNA with bananas . . .

GORILLA

Chin scratcher

If you compare a human skull and a gorilla skull, you might notice that the area under the gorilla's mouth slopes back towards the neck. Humans are the only animals that we know of that have chins. Scientists are still trying to work out why this is!

HUMAN

FRUITY FEAST
Do gorillas eat bananas?

Apes love to eat all kinds of fruits in the forest. However, though you might see gorillas eating bananas on TV or in zoos, they don't often eat them in the wild. They can eat bananas, but just don't have that many opportunities to find them!

Gorillas are herbivores, which means they mostly eat plants. This is unusual for such large and muscly animals. Western gorillas have been spotted eating the occasional insect, but they mostly stick to leaves, shoots, stems, fruits, and flowers.

No meat thanks

Although old stories were told of angry, man-eating gorillas, they weren't true. Unlike chimpanzees—who occasionally eat other animals (including other chimps!)—gorillas never engage in this kind of behavior. It's plants all the way!

Seasonal selection

Chimps love to eat figs and wild pineapples. They also like sugarcane, jackfruit, and mango, although these are not part of their natural diet. They'll eat whatever fruit is growing in season where they live.

Bonobo brunch

Bonobos are omnivores, which means they eat a mixture of plants and animals. Although half of their diet is fruit, they also eat seeds, leaves, stems, shoots, flowers, fungus, and even honey. They also like foraging in swamps and streams for aquatic plants. Researchers have seen them eat shrimp and bugs, like caterpillars and worms.

Pong perfect

Orangutans love eating the spiky durian fruit that grows in Indonesia. It's famous for being extremely smelly—something like rotting meat and smelly old socks. Nice!

Dinner time

In zoos, gorillas' favorite foods are berries, guavas, and pith, which is a tough tissue found in the stems of certain flowering plants. In the wild, eastern gorillas in particular eat a lot of leaves, as fruit is pretty scarce in their habitats. They can even stomach nettles and thistles!

WATCH OUT
Why is poop important?

When you walk through the forest, watch where you step! You don't want a sticky surprise...

"Scat" is what rangers and scientists call animal poop. Some people spend years researching scat to learn more about the animal it came from. Yes, that's right... animal poop is awesome!

Pooper interesting

Scientists collect and study scat to learn more about animal populations. Scat can help them identify the animals that have been in a certain area, and how long ago. It also contains an enormous amount of other useful information: how stressed the animals are, who they are related to, their feeding behaviors, and other clues about their happiness and health.

Scat-tastic!

Apes eat a lot of fruit and leaves—sometimes as much as 45 lb. a day! So a good poop is a moist poop. Gorillas poop every few hours. It's usually quite soft and varies in color from light to dark brown.

Happy tummy

Because apes eat a lot of fruit, they burp and fart a lot too! Gorillas have big round bellies filled with a lot of intestines to help them process all the food they eat.

POOP CHART

For apes in captivity, researchers have a poop-scoring index which they use to check the animals' health. If their poop is too hard or too runny there could be problems with the food they're being fed or how the animal is feeling. Paying attention to poop can make everyone happier. A little gross maybe, but helpful!

1.
2.
3.
4.
5.
6.
7.

FAMILY MATTERS

How do apes live?

Different species of apes have different kinds of family life. Most apes live in groups, in a certain part of a forest or jungle. This is known as their "territory." A gorilla's territory can cover a large area, as groups will travel long distances to search for food. Gorilla territories usually overlap with those of other groups, but they try to avoid bumping into each other!

Gather round!

Male orangutans are very solitary, preferring to live alone. Gorillas form groups of ten or less. Bonobos live in big, mixed groups of thirty to eighty apes. Chimpanzee groups are the largest—in Uganda, researchers have recorded communities with nearly two hundred individuals!

Who's in charge?

Adult male gorillas are known as "silverbacks" because they have—you guessed it—silver backs. Males can start to develop a saddle-shaped patch of silvery-gray hair on their backs at around twelve years old, although some develop it later. The biggest and strongest silverback in a troop is usually the boss of the group.

Chill out!
Gorillas are generally very calm-natured, although they will stand up for themselves if threatened. Chimp society is male-dominated and quite aggressive. Bonobos in captivity are famous for being peaceful and relaxed, but fights do happen in the wild. In bonobo society, males and females can both be leaders, although males won't get far without their mothers' support.

Group names
You have probably heard of a flock of birds or a herd of cows. Well, a group of chimpanzees or bonobos is called a "community." They can also form smaller groups within a community called "parties." Gorillas form "troops" or "bands." There are also "buffooneries" of orangutans!

MOM KNOWS BEST
Do apes care for each other?

Ape mothers are very caring and are naturally protective of their children. Young apes are called babies or infants, and they need a lot of help in the early stages of their lives.

Taxi service

For the first five months of its life, a baby chimp is carried everywhere by its mom and clings tightly to her hair. They can begin to walk and climb at about six months old. The baby is dependent on its mom for at least two years—but sometimes rides on her back for fun even as a four-year-old!

Baby steps

Chimpanzees usually only give birth every three or four years. A first-time mother takes a little while to get the hang of things, but there are usually a lot of other moms in the community to watch and learn from.

Ongoing job

As the chimps grow up to become teenagers, the moms still play a big role in teaching and guiding them. They offer comfort, reassurance, and support. Research has shown that when chimp moms are more present in the lives of their sons, their chances of success are greater!

Playtime

Young chimps play with each other and are very interested in the forest. Sometimes they find "toys" like a feather, or even other animals. Bonobos have been observed catching little monkeys and mongooses and playing with them like pets or possessions. This doesn't usually end well for the "toy" though!

Milkshake baby

Baby gorillas weigh around 4.5 lb. when they are born—by the time they are adults they can weigh up to 500 lb.! Baby gorillas feed almost entirely on their mom's milk for about three years, before moving on to eating fruits and leaves.

FIELD WORK

Can you study the apes?

The study of apes is called "primatology." People from all kinds of backgrounds now make science and conservation their aim. Being a field researcher requires a lot of patience, as well as bravery—the forest is full of challenges.

The "Trimates" are three amazing women who researched apes in their natural environments in the 1960s and 70s. They have inspired so many others to follow in their footsteps, but they couldn't have carried out their work without the support and knowledge of local communities.

Dian Fossey

Dian Fossey founded a gorilla research camp at Karisoke in Rwanda in 1967, between two volcanoes. She became known by locals as Nyiramachabelli which means, "the woman who lives alone on the mountain."

D. Fossey

J. Goodall

Jane Goodall

Jane Goodall went to Gombe National Park in Tanzania in 1960. She has dedicated her whole life to protecting chimpanzees and was one of the first people to describe them using "tools," such as fishing for termites with twigs.

B. Galdikas

Birutė Galdikas

Birutė Galdikas arrived in Borneo in 1971 and battled snakes, spiders, leeches, and constant rain to set up camp. Her hardest task was finding wild orangutans, as they are so shy and solitary.

How to greet a gorilla

- Bow and make yourself as small as possible.
- Stay quiet and calm.
- Never go near the babies in the troop.
- Always stay with your guide.

SCREEN TIME

Are gorillas really monsters?

Some movies tell strange—and often negative—stories about apes. Gorillas are not giant monkeys! They are not monkeys at all. They are also not ferocious beasts—they are mostly gentle and shy. They are not predators or man-eaters—they love leaves, fruits, and flowers. And they definitely do not climb skyscrapers or fight dinosaurs!

Take two!

Thankfully, new movies are being made to tell different kinds of stories. A documentary about broadcaster David Attenborough visiting endangered mountain gorillas at a sanctuary in Rwanda helped to educate people and change their opinions about these wonderful animals.

Ape ads

Apes and monkeys of all kinds have also been used in advertising. You may have seen them on TV and in magazines to make people laugh and buy things—from cars to tea and chocolate! Is it right to use animals to sell things?

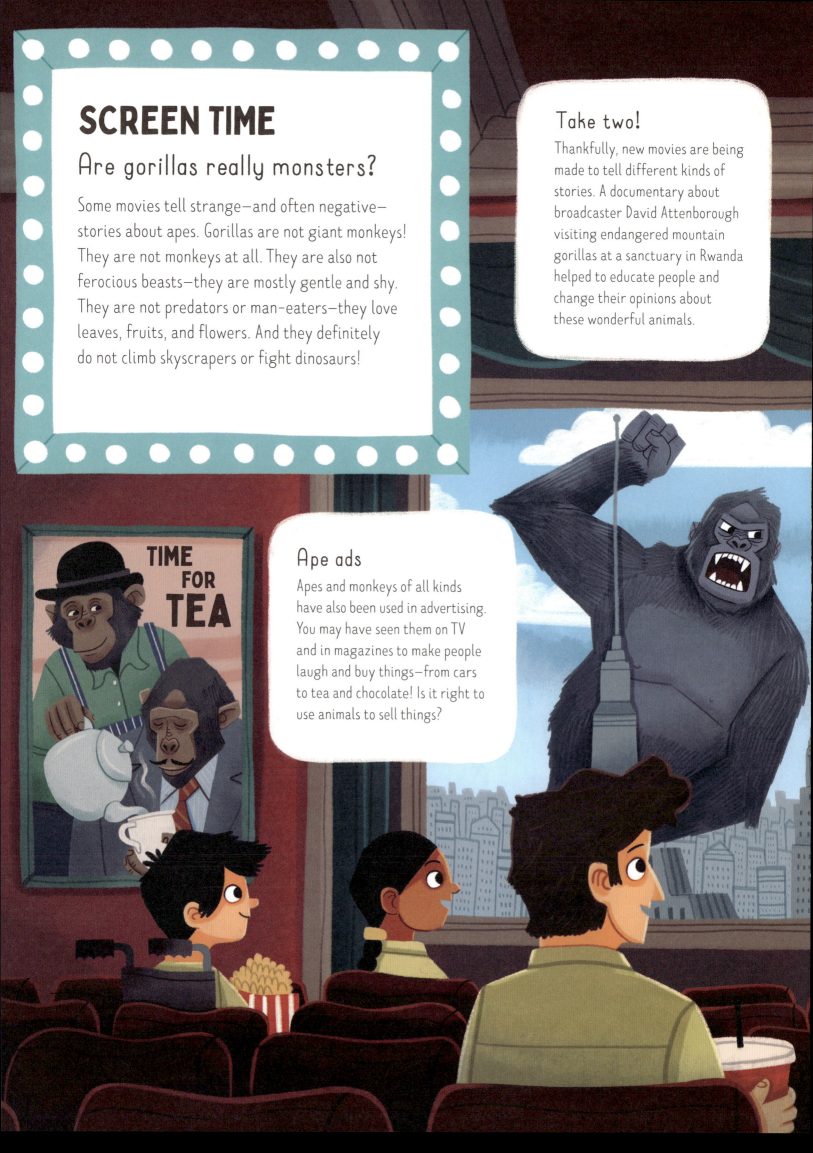

Time for change
Unlike humans, apes don't dream of being a star on the screen. To them, acting is stressful and confusing. There is no reason to use live apes in movies or advertising now that technology is so advanced. Many movies, like *The Lion King* and *Jurassic Park*, have used computers to create all kinds of realistic animals.

Making myths
Long before movies were even invented, people were already telling stories about apes that made them sound dangerous or evil. Today, myths like the Yeti and Bigfoot continue to mix truth with scary fiction. Can you think of any other myths or stories that paint creatures in a bad light?

BEAUTIFUL BRAINS
Do gorillas get grumpy?

Based on how closely humans and nonhuman apes are related, scientists are always researching how they behave, and trying to understand how their brains work. We can be fairly sure that apes are able to feel emotions such as fear, hunger, boredom, and happiness—just like us!

Clever creatures
Apes are highly intelligent creatures. It was previously thought that only humans build knowledge with each generation, but apes do too. They pass information from one individual to another, with younger apes learning skills for surviving in their habitats from elders.

Dreamtime

Some people have nightmares about creatures they are afraid of—including gorillas. But do gorillas have bad dreams too? And what are they most afraid of? We don't know for sure, but new research is helping us understand more about their sleep habits. We do know that gorillas like to sleep together in nests made out of foliage. They have also been observed cooperating with chimpanzees to keep watch for nighttime threats, like leopards!

Humanlike

"Anthropomorphism" is a word that is used when human traits, ideas, and emotions are given to nonhuman creatures or things. This is often applied to animals, as we imagine them to look or act like us. Imagining how animals are feeling can help people to connect with them, and become curious to know more about their natural behaviors. That said, it's important to remember that animals experience the world in very different ways to us, and often don't have the same needs.

HANDY SKILLS

Are gorillas really strong?

Gorillas have huge hands. They also have opposable thumbs, just like us. This means they can grasp branches, peel apart tough stems, and carefully pluck fruits and flowers. Even better than humans, they also have semi-opposable feet! Their big toe is long and very flexible, giving them extra abilities for grabbing things and climbing.

Giant gorillas

While gorillas usually move about "quadrupedally," with four limbs on the ground, when they stand up they are over 5.5 ft. tall. Did you know that a human's height is usually equal to the length of their outstretched arm span? Gorillas, on the other hand, have a longer arm-length to height ratio. Their arm span averages about 8 ft. long!

Group hug

Apes spend a lot of time grooming each other with their gentle hands. They love cuddling, touching, and picking dirt and bugs from each other's hair. Gentle touches build trust and bonds between them.

Pure power

A gorilla punch can exert up to 2,700 lb. of force—a trained boxer can exert about 750 lb.! Gorillas' muscles are also up to four times stronger than the chunkiest of human bodybuilders. They are able to pull small trees over to get to the fruit and rip bark off trunks. Seriously strong!

Koko speaks

Gorillas can use their hands for other things too. Koko, a western gorilla born at San Francisco Zoo, was taught sign language signs as part of a research project in the 1970s. She learned more than one thousand signs and could understand more than two thousand words of spoken English! She appeared on the cover of *National Geographic* twice and was named the "most important gorilla that ever lived."

LISTEN UP
How do apes talk?

Apes communicate with each other in special ways. We may not be able to understand their calls, but they are able to understand each other perfectly.

Chimpanzees are the noisiest apes. They use many different sounds to communicate, such as grunts, hoots, screeches, and whimpers. Gorillas are generally quiet animals, but they may bark, grunt, and roar. They also like to chuckle and burp! When it's feeding time, some gorillas even hum!

Gorilla sounds
Dian Fossey has described sixteen different vocalization types from gorillas. She classified the sounds into categories with different purposes, ranging from babies needing help from their mothers, to young males showing off how strong they are!

Apes also communicate through physical gestures. They have over one hundred different types, which they use like a language.

CLEVER AND COOL

How smart are chimpanzees?

Chimpanzees are very intelligent and pretty cool too! Did you know that some chimps admire leaves like works of art? We sometimes think chimps are naughty, but they really are just noisy and very curious about the world.

Tool use

Chimps do all sorts of awesome things. They have been studied using rocks to crack open hard panda nuts, and making spears out of sticks, which they sharpen with their teeth. They have also been seen using leaves as sponges to help them drink water and fermented plant juice.

Space chimps

In 1961, a chimpanzee named Ham was strapped into a rocket and sent on a suborbital flight into space. Later that year, another chimp named Enos made a flight all the way around Earth! These missions helped scientists learn more about space travel and how to make it safe for humans, but many people now think sending animals into space was cruel.

New medicine
New field observations have even shown chimpanzees caring for scratches and wounds on their bodies by catching insects, squeezing them in their lips and then applying them to their cuts. Elsewhere, orangutans have also been seen applying plant materials to soothe muscle injuries. Incredible apes!

Not so cool
Being so closely related to humans, chimpanzees have often been used for research in laboratories—to study diseases, brain function, and more. Many countries have now banned using apes for this purpose, but macaques and smaller monkeys like marmosets and tamarins are still being used. Is it right to use animals in this way?

BIG THREATS

Are apes in danger?

Sadly, the answer is yes. Apes are threatened by many different things. Orangutans face huge problems because of the global desire for palm oil. Gorillas in Africa are under threat too, from mining, logging, and poaching.

Palm oil problem

Palm oil—also called *Elaeis guineensis*—comes from the fruit of oil palm trees. If you squeeze the fleshy fruit it produces crude palm oil, and if you crush the stone in the middle of the fruit it produces palm kernel oil.

Almost half of the packaged products you find in a supermarket will contain palm oil—from pizza and chocolate, to shampoo and toothpaste! Collecting palm oil to use in products like these is leading to the destruction of many forests around the world.

Bad news

In some African cultures, people still eat chimpanzee and gorilla meat. There are also poachers who will shoot adult apes and capture the babies to sell as pets. Poachers often sell gorilla body parts too—some people think they are like magic charms and might make the human that owns them more powerful.

Ranger champions

In the Virunga National Park in the Congo, there are more than seven hundred rangers working to stop illegal poaching activity. Some rangers have even been killed by poachers when trying to protect the mountain gorillas.

Safe sanctuaries

There are now many sanctuaries in different countries for rescued orphan gorillas, chimps, and orangutans whose mothers have been killed by poachers. Over time, some of the orphans could be released back into the wild.

TROUBLED TIMES
Will apes go extinct?

All apes, except for humans, are endangered. They have already become locally extinct in many of the areas where they used to live, due to forests being cleared for settlement, agriculture, and business. Though shooting or capturing apes is illegal in many countries, these laws are difficult to enforce.

Orangutans are under the biggest threat. In total, across the three species, there may be fewer than 100,000 of these amazing apes left on the planet—though their population was once numbered in the millions.

TAPANULI ORANGUTAN
ONLY 800 LEFT

The Tapanuli orangutan, *Pongo tapanuliensis*, is only found in a single, high, mountain forest called Batang Toru in Sumatra. They are cut off from other orangutans.

CROSS RIVER GORILLA
ONLY 200 LEFT

The Cross River gorilla, *Gorilla gorilla diehli*, is a subspecies of the western gorilla, scattered among ten family groups in rainforests on the border of Nigeria and Cameroon. Scientists haven't been able to study them much because they inhabit rugged territory and are wary of people.

THE RAREST PRIMATE
ONLY 25 LEFT

The world's rarest primate is a gibbon. The Hainan gibbon, *Nomascus hainanus*, is only found in the Bawangling Nature Reserve on a tropical island off the southern coast of China. There are possibly only twenty-five individuals left, which might not be enough to keep the population alive.

Pay attention
Animals that are said to be critically endangered are very likely to become extinct in the near future, unless we act fast. Extinction means that all members of a species have died and the animals are gone forever. This cannot be allowed to happen!

HAPPY ALONE
What do orangutans like most?

Orangutans are very shy apes and spend almost all of their lives in the trees. Male orangutans prefer a solitary life and don't really spend much time with their families at all. They are perfectly designed for life in the treetops: mostly hanging from branches, and eating. They are happy to be left alone!

Size difference

Like many other primates, male and female orangutans look quite different from one another. This is called "sexual dimorphism." Male orangutans are almost twice as large as females!

Big boomers

As males get older, they grow beards, and their body hair gets longer. Their cheeks swell and grow into pads called "flanges." The flanges amplify the rumbling calls they can make, which boom out loudly across the forest. The bigger the flanges, the more attractive the males are to female orangutans, and the more impressive they are to other males.

Special baby
Orangutans are very slow breeders—they produce on average just one baby every eight years. This is why hunting and habitat loss are especially dangerous for them.

Searching for home
When male orangutans reach maturity at about ten-years-old, they leave the area where they were born and establish territories of their own. This has become a lot harder as much of their forest habitat has been destroyed.

Did you know?
When Charles Darwin was working on his big idea that humans and other animals are related, he was fascinated by an orangutan in London Zoo. She was called Jenny. Darwin praised her intelligence and she got him thinking in new ways.

FINDING HOPE
How can we help apes?

Our message is simple: humans must learn to share this planet with other animals. We need to coexist happily and peacefully for conservation to be successful. Though humans can be destructive, we are also clever, and have the potential to do fabulous things. There are many people around the world trying to help apes.

Forest guardians

Protecting habitats is the best way to ensure animals have a future. If the forests are protected, apes will continue to recover.

Support charities

There are many charities working hard to improve the future for apes. They are helping to protect habitats from deforestation and put a stop to poaching. A big part of conservation is raising awareness of the problems that animals are facing, and many charities work with people from local communities near where apes live to help find solutions to suit everyone. Will you stand up for apes too?

Future zoos

If you were in charge of a zoo, in what ways could you improve the lives of apes? Zoos help with conservation projects and breeding programs as well as being great places to learn more about animals. But many people think keeping animals in captivity is unfair. Do you think we need zoos?

Too much stuff

Another way to help apes is to think carefully about the products we buy. Most cell phones and laptops now include a metal ore called coltan, which has been mined in Central Africa, destroying gorilla habitats. Please recycle as much as you can!

Join in

September 24th has been declared "World Gorilla Day," and each year many charities and zoos run "Ape Awareness" events all through the month of April (or Ape-ril!). You can join in the fun by having your own ape party or raising money to support conservation projects.

APE WORDS

ARCHAEOLOGISTS: Scientists and historians who study the ancient remains of humans and their cultures.

CLIMATE CHANGE: Long-term changes in global temperatures and weather patterns. These are caused not only by natural processes but also by human activity, including burning fossil fuels such as coal and oil.

COMMON ANCESTOR: An animal or plant from which other species of animals or plants has evolved.

CONSERVATION: Protecting animals and nature.

ENDANGERED: May soon no longer exist.

EVOLUTION: The gradual change of a species over time, usually in ways that make it better able to survive and reproduce.

EXTINCTION: When a species of animal or plant no longer exists.

FORAGING: Searching for food in the wild.

GROOMING: When an animal cleans itself or others. Primates often help groom each other.

HABITAT: The natural environment of an animal or plant species.

MAMMALS: Animals that have hair on their bodies and nurse their young with milk.

OMNIVORE: An animal that eats a mixture of plants and other animals.

PREDATOR: An animal that kills or eats other animals.

PRIMATE: A group of mammals with hands that can grasp objects, which includes apes, monkeys, lemurs, and tarsiers.

PRIMATOLOGY: The study of primates by scientists.

RAINFOREST: A thick forest habitat that stays wet all year round.

SANCTUARY: A protected location where rescued animals can live and be looked after by humans if they cannot live safely in the wild.

SCAT: Animal poop.

SPECIES: A group of animals or plants that can breed together.

SOLITARY: Used to describe an animal that prefers to live alone.

TERRITORY: An area of land where an animal or group of animals live, and which they defend from intruders of the same species.

VOCALIZATIONS: Sounds made by animals to communicate with each other or send messages to other animals.

INDEX

A
ancestors 14–15, 16–17, 46
anthropomorphism 31
archaeologists 16

B
bonobos 10, 12, 17, 22–23, 25

C
chimpanzees 6–7, 10, 12, 17, 16, 22, 23, 24–25, 31, 34, 36–37, 39
climate change 14
communication 34–35
conservation 26–27, 44–45, 46

D
Darwin, Charles 43

E
emotions 30–31
endangered animals 12–13, 40–41, 46
evolution 16, 46
extinction 40–41, 46

F
families 22–23, 24–25
food 16–17, 21
Fossey, Dian 26, 34
fruit 16–17, 20–21, 38

G
Galdikas, Birutė 27
gibbons 10–11, 41
Goodall, Jane 26
gorillas 6–7, 8–9, 11, 17, 22–23, 26–27, 32–33, 34–35, 39, 45
  Cross River gorillas 40
  eastern gorillas 8, 12, 17
  western gorillas 8, 10, 12, 40
grooming 33

H
habitats 6–7, 9, 43, 44–45, 46
humans 8, 9, 10–11, 16–17, 32–33

L
Linnaeus, Carl 10

M
monkeys 10, 14–15, 28, 37

O
orangutans 6–7, 8, 13, 17, 22–23, 27, 37, 38, 39, 40, 42–43
  Bornean orangutans 10, 13
  Sumatran orangutans 13
  Tapanuli orangutans 40

P
palm oil 38
poaching 38–39
poop 20–21
predators 12, 46
primates 4, 10, 14–15, 46
primatology 26–27, 46

S
sanctuaries 9, 39, 46
scat 20–21, 46
silverbacks 22, 35
small apes 11
space 36
species 8–9, 11, 12–13, 40–41, 46

T
territory 22, 46
"Trimates" 26–27
troops 22–23

V
vocalization 34–35, 46

For Nell, my favorite ape. —Huw

For Ciara and Simone, the cheekiest chimps I know. —Sam

Do Gorillas Eat Bananas? © 2025 Thames & Hudson Ltd, London

Concept and Text © 2025 Huw Lewis Jones
Illustrations © 2025 Sam Caldwell

Additional consultancy by Catherine Hobaiter

All Rights Reserved. No part of this publication may be reproduced or transmitted in any form or by any means, electronic or mechanical, including photocopy, recording or any other information storage and retrieval system, without prior permission in writing from the publisher.

First published in the United States of America in 2025 by
Thames & Hudson Inc., 500 Fifth Avenue, New York, New York 10110

EU Authorized Representative: Interart S.A.R.L.
19 rue Charles Auray, 93500 Pantin, Paris, France
productsafety@thameshudson.co.uk
www.interart.fr

Library of Congress Control Number 2024933375

ISBN 978-0-500-65323-4
01

Printed and bound in China by C & C Offset Printing Co. Ltd

Be the first to know about our new releases,
exclusive content and author events by visiting
thamesandhudson.com
thamesandhudsonusa.com
thamesandhudson.com.au